The P____ __ ___rds
Speaking Life Into Our Children

Proverbs 18:21 Death and life are in the power of the tongue...

Shawn M. McBride

(The Power of Words: Speaking Life Into Our Children)
Copyright © 2015 by Shawn Maurice McBride

ISBN-13:
978-1514330388

ISBN-10:
1514330385

About The Author

A native of Washington, DC Shawn McBride is a phenomenal and dynamic national youth speaker. He has become a best-selling author of three books geared towards America's youth: *Beware of Bad Company*, *Know Your Worth* and *How To Become A Successful Student*. For over two decades, he has faithfully served hundreds of thousands young people and families in over 30 US states. He creatively and passionately speaks to the younger generation, parents and adult youth workers in public schools, private schools and in various denominations.

TABLE OF CONTENTS

INTRODUCTION

"Death and life are in the power of the tongue..."
– Proverbs 18:21 (NKJV)

Several years ago I was invited to speak to a group of 60 high school students. My plan was to give a message about the affects of our words in order to do my part in discouraging bullying. As you know, so many young people in recent years have committed suicide and harmed themselves because of bullying. Before I proceeded into the content of the talk I wrote this phrase on the dry erase board that was hanging on the wall:

Death and life are in the power of the tongue...

As we repeated this phrase in unison several times I gave each student a blank sheet of paper and asked them to list only DEATH WORDS that they have heard at home from their parents or guardians within the past six months. I instructed them to only write down the phrases and words that seemed to be negative, demeaning and made them feel upset. I told them to be completely honest and that they could remain totally anonymous.

Once this introductory assignment was complete and the papers were collected and handed over to me I was completely blown away, shocked and honestly quite appalled at what these young high school students wrote. What I am about to share with you has become the basis and foundation of me writing this book:

What 60 High School Students Shared With Me About Death Words They Are Hearing From Parents/Guardians:

- "I know you can try harder."
- "What's wrong with you?"
- "You can't do anything right."
- "Why can't you be more like your sibling?"
- "You were a mistake."
- "Why can't you just listen?"
- "Are you stupid?"

It is my goal through this writing to enlighten and educate parents, guardians and those who work with young people about the positive and negative affects our words have on kids and teens. This subject matter is crucial. Several years have passed since that original talk with the 60 high school students. I have had countless opportunities to speak with literally thousands of young people all across the U.S. to prove and crystalize my thesis. My own personal and daily interaction with my five children has proved effective as well in applying the concepts, principles and ideals that I will share with you.

Shawn McBride, Washington DC Summer 2015

CHAPTER ONE

THE POWER OF AFFIRMING WORDS

Denzel Washington is arguably one of the greatest actors of all time. He has played almost every character imaginable and has become one of the highest paid actors in Hollywood. He is also a film producer. Not long ago, I read a fascinating story about one of the most important motivating factors that caused him to want to pursue acting as a career. It had everything to do with the power of words.

My second go-round at Fordham I switched to the school's midtown campus where they had a real drama program, and I became passionate about acting. Bob Stone, my English teacher, was involved in the theater program and knew his stuff. He'd been on Broadway with stars like Paul Robeson and Jose Ferrer and had accomplished a lot. I told him I was serious about becoming an actor and he encouraged me. More than that, he believed in me. After I appeared in a student production of Othello he wrote a letter of recommendation for me to grad school. What he basically said was, "If you don't have the talent to nurture this young man, then don't accept him." I must've read that letter a hundred times. Each time I thought, Wow! If he thinks I'm that good then I'm going to have to live up to those words. He put a fire under me. For years I kept that letter in my pocket — I still have it. Whenever things became tough, I read it. There were times I wondered if I'd ever catch my first break, but Bob's words kept me going..."

Everybody needs encouragement, including famous people like Denzel Washington! What amazes me the most about his story is that he read and re-read the letter over and over again. Reading the letter one time would not do. He even kept the letter with him for years and used it as personal motivation. I suspect that Denzel needed the motivation from others to believe in himself. This is why he said: *"Wow! If he thinks I'm that good then I'm going to have to live up to those words. He put a fire under me."*

You see, as human beings we all have a desire and need to be acknowledged for who we are. We need to know that who we are is good enough. That we can make it. This is no different for our children. Children need to know that they can indeed accomplish certain things. When we give children positive words of affirmation it tells them they are good enough. It tells them they are deserving and worthy.

When I speak of positive words of affirmation I am speaking specifically about POSITIVE LIFE WORDS.

- Speaking positive words to a child that will instill a positive attitude and outlook no matter what circumstances they are experiencing in the present or in the past.
- Speaking encouraging and inspirational words to a child that will lift up their spirit.
- Speaking empowering words to a child that will improve their lives.
- Speaking thoughtful, confident, words to a child that will offer them hope.

I have seen with my own eyes the incredible power of speaking POSITVE LIFE WORDS to young people and the effects it has on them emotionally.

I will never forget the time I spoke positive words of affirmation to a little eight-year-old boy who I met in Texas a few years ago. After I finished speaking I was standing at the exit door shaking hands, taking selfies with strangers and greeting people as they departed the event. This little bright-eyed and bushy tailed kind of kid came up to me to shake my hand. I stooped down so that I could be on his level and make eye contact with him. I said these words with a sense of boldness and confidence:

"Young man, you are special! You are a handsome fellow and you have greatness inside of you. You will

10

one day make a huge difference in the lives of many people. You are special!"

You should have seen the look on his face! He turned fireball red, smiled as wide as the Grand Canyon, ran over to his mother and said:

"Mom, that man told me that I was special and that I have greatness inside of me and that one day I am going to make a difference!"

I sincerely believe that my positive words of affirmation inflated and ignited something in this child's spirit. He was so excited and energized by the words I spoke that he could hardly contain himself.

I suspect that there are so many kids in this world including our own that potentially would be so incredibly inspired, encouraged and feel a sense of hope if we just took the time to speak positive words of affirmation into their lives. I firmly believe that when you CHANGE your words, you can change a life!

CHAPTER TWO

WORDS ARE SEEDS

"Words are seeds they land in our hearts and not the ground. Be careful what you plant and careful what you say. You might have to eat what you planted one day."
– Ritu Ghatourey

My heart is deeply burdened today for the loss of parenting skills in this generation of parents. So many parents do not understand that the words we speak into the lives our children will mold and shape them.

Our words are like seeds being planted into the little garden of a child's heart and have so much power in them. A good gardener knows how important it is to plant the right kind of seeds into fertile soil so they will become healthy plants, beautiful flowers, thick bushes and strong trees.

Our words are seeds that are being planted in their young hearts and minds that will grow, develop and impact them for the rest of their lives. It is crucial as parents and adults who care about young people that we are intentional about planting life-giving words, rather than death words, into their hearts.

When we plant these kinds of positive life-giving seeds into our children, in the course of time the seeds will germinate and produce plants of self confidence, bushes of self-esteem, flowers of internal happiness and beautiful trees of success.

Whatever information, whether in the form of hardware or software, is installed inside of a computer will be processed by that computer. Hundreds of thousands of pieces of information will be stored and retrieved as needed. This is exactly how a child's mind works. Their minds are just like a CPU. Whether it's a young child or a teenage child, the mind is very active and has hundreds of thousands of thoughts running through it each and every day. These thoughts are stored and retrieved as needed. Future situations will be influenced by the negative or positive thoughts they have saved.

In addition to a computer, the minds of our children are like a tape recorder that is always on and recording without intermission. As the tape recorder is operating it is recording everything that is happening in a child's life whether positive or negative, happy or sad, good or bad. It is recording everything that child sees though images and especially hears through words. The tape recorder has the ability not only to record, but to also play back those experiences. Because of a lack of maturity, a child will eventually imitate the images and words they see and hear.

It is important to note that it is impossible to change or erase any unpleasant and negative experiences that have taken place in a child's life. It's recorded forever, however, as parents and adults who work with kids, we have the power to record over the negative experiences by speaking positive words of affirmation into their lives. In other words, the positive, encouraging, confident and inspiring words that we speak to them eventually will record over the negative thought tapes with new positive thoughts. Positive words of affirmations like:

- "I believe in you!"
- "I love you!"
- "You are special!"
- "You are a beautiful young lady!"

Dr. John Trent who is the Vice President of Today's Family wrote an article years ago that illustrates that power of words of affirmation on one young girl in particular:

Mary had grown up knowing that she was different from the other kids, and she hated it. She was born with a cleft palate and had to bear the jokes and stares of cruel children who teased her non-stop about her misshaped lip, crooked nose, and garbled speech.

With all the teasing, Mary grew up hating the fact that she was "different." She was convinced that no one, outside her family, could ever love her... until she entered Mrs. Leonard's class.

Mrs. Leonard had a warm smile, a round face, and shiny brown hair. While everyone in her class liked her, Mary came to love Mrs. Leonard.

In the 1950's, it was common for teachers to give their children an annual hearing test. However, in Mary's case, in addition to her cleft palate, she was barely able to hear out of one ear. Determined not to let the other children have another "difference" to point out, she would cheat on the test each year. The "whisper test" was given by having a child walk to the classroom door, turn sideways, close one ear with a finger, and then repeat something, which the teacher whispered.

Mary turned her bad ear towards her teacher and pretended to cover her good ear. She knew that teachers would often say things like, "The sky is blue," or "What color are your shoes?"

But not on that day. Surely, God put seven words in Mrs. Leonard's mouth that changed Mary's life forever. When the "Whisper test" came, Mary heard the words: "I wish you were my little girl."

Dads, I wish there was some way that I could communicate to you the incredible blessing which affirming words impart to children. I wish, too, that you could sit in my office, when I counsel, and hear the terrible damage that individuals received from not hearing affirming words – particularly affirming words from a father. While words from a godly teacher can melt a heart, words from a father can powerfully set the course of a life.

If affirming words were something rarely spoken in your home growing up, let me give you some tips on words and phrases that can brighten your own child's eyes and life. These words are easy to say to any child who comes into your life. I'm proud of you, Way to go, Bingo … you did it, Magnificent, I knew you could do it, What a good helper, You're very special to me, I trust you, What a treasure, Hurray for you, Beautiful work, You're a real trooper, Well done, That's so creative, You make my day, You're a joy, Give me a big hug, You're such a good listener, You figured it out, I love you, You're so responsible, You remembered, You're the best, You sure tried hard,

I've got to hand it to you, I couldn't be prouder of you, You light up my day, I'm praying for you, You're wonderful, I'm behind you, You're so kind to your (brother/sister), You're God's special gift, I'm here for you.

John Trent, Ph.D., Vice President of Today's Family, Men of Action, Winter 1993, p. 5

Parents and those who take care of children should take the time to plant good or positive seeds in their children so they will grow and flourish. How many parents spend as much time preparing for a child as they do planting a garden? Sadly, most parents don't prepare at all and they just rely on the parenting skills that have been taught by their parents, which may not have been very good at all. This means that the parents will speak the same death words and send the same demeaning messages to their children that they grew up with. They don't mean to, but they aren't intentionally trying to change the cycle and patterns they were taught.

Brenda J. Silveira published an article called *Planting Positive Seeds in Your Children* in 2013 on ezinearticles.com that explains the difference of parents planting positive and negative seeds in children:

Have people planted positive or negative seeds in your garden? Are you planting positive or negative seeds?

Positive seeds create positive thoughts, which create positive words and actions, which create positive results. On the other hand, negative seeds create negative thoughts, which create negative words and actions, which bring negative results.

In order to make our garden of life beautiful, we have to determine what kind of seeds have been planted in our garden. Then we have to make sure that we start planting positive seeds, both in ourselves and others.

Each word you speak has much more weight when you realize that you are always planting a seed. The seed may take years to mature and you may not see the full outcome until after a child is grown, but know that every word you speak can either help a child to produce fruit or slowly kill their spirit.

CHAPTER THREE

YOU CAN'T TAKE IT BACK

*"Those who control their tongue will have a long
life; opening your mouth can ruin everything."*
– Proverbs 13:3 (NLT)

Once while teaching a class I was trying to explain to
a group of children the ability of words to hurt people,
especially those we love. I used a fresh tube of
toothpaste to show what happens when we speak
negative words about people. Every time I said
something mean I would squeeze the tube onto a
paper towel until finally the tube was empty. I then
asked one of the children to put the toothpaste back
into the tube. He quickly realized that would not be
possible. I explained that once we've said bad things
about people it is not possible to *"take our words
back."*

Sometimes words are said out of anger, and we find
that it can be impossible to take words back after they
are said, much like trying to put toothpaste back in the
tube after it's been squeezed out.

We have all uttered something and instantly wished
we had practiced more self-control and kept it to

ourselves. Sometimes the instant we hear the words coming out of our mouths, we already know we made a mistake. Other times it can take several days, months or even years before we realize the mistake. Moments of frustration, anger or sadness weaken our ability to manage what we say. Sadly, these are the times we need to exercise the most self-control. Feelings and emotions are heightened and you are much more likely to say something that should have never crossed your lips in the first place.

You love your children and you would never intentionally harm them, but your words spoken in the heat of the moment can absolutely do some major damage. What kind of things are we talking about?

- *"You are so stupid!"*
- *"How can you be so dumb?"*
- *"You are awful!"*
- *"I hate you when you act like this."*
- *"I wish you were more like _____."*
- *"You make my life miserable."*

Some of those phrases are said without real meaning, but the words are just as harsh. Children are very literal creatures in their early years, which makes every word you say very real to them. As kids grow into adolescence and go through puberty, they tend to be very moody, sensitive and have poor self-esteem simply because of the hormones and changes they are going through. When a parent says something that is hurtful, intentional or not, those are the words the child remembers. A hundred different praises can be wiped out with one, hurtful phrase that can never be taken back.

Judgment Day

How important are our words? We must give an account of every idle word that we speak in our lifetime. St. Matthew 12:36-37 (KJV) says, *"But I say unto you, That every idle word that men shall speak, they shall give account thereof in the day of judgment. 37For by thy words thou shalt be justified, and by thy words thou shalt be condemned."*

We need to define what "idle" means in order to get a complete understanding of what this verse means. The word "idle" means inactive, unemployed, barren, useless, lazy, and slow. That means every word that we speak that is unproductive, unfruitful, and unspiritual, we must give an account of it. Does that mean every sarcastic comment, every racial joke, every unfounded criticism, and every profanity? It certainly does mean just that. I can see why Jesus said in his sermon on the mount in St. Matthew 5:37 (KJV), *"But let your communication be, Yea, yea; Nay, nay: for whatsoever is more than these cometh of evil."*

Wow! We all have work to do in this area because our words are more than just what is spoken. What we write and share on social media (yes, Facebook too!) counts. God has a good reason for addressing idle words so heavily in the Bible.

Hurtful Words Leave Holes

There is a story that was once told about a young boy who had a tendency to blow up and say hurtful things when he was angry. Despite the parents' efforts, they couldn't get him to see just how hurtful those words were. One day, the dad brings the boy a hammer and nails. He tells the boy to go out to the back fence and drive 100 nails into the fence randomly. The boy does and then the father tells the boy to go remove all the nails from the fence. The boy does. The nails are gone, but the wood is filled with holes.

When we say hurtful things or words that should never be said in the first place, we may apologize, but the damage doesn't go away. It is there. It leaves a scar. The words have done the damage and although the person who was hurt won't show it, the pain is there.

The words, like the holes in the fence, take a little something away each time. Every time a nail was driven into that wood, it was chipping away, weakening the board. When you say words in anger or grief, they make their mark on the child's psyche. Angry, hurtful words don't always have to be directed at the child to do damage.

If you and your spouse get into a heated argument, things may be said that the child hears. The child will remember those words. Those words will foster feelings of anger, sadness or even defiance against one or both parents. What many parents tend to forget is the fact that kids, especially young ones, are like sponges. They absorb everything. Have you ever been watching your child play and a toy breaks or blocks fall over and your child utters a word they shouldn't be saying? Where do you think that word came from? It's a learned response. Your child watches you and listens to you. They quickly pick up how to respond to something that frustrates them or angers them. They use YOUR words—not theirs.

As the children get older, they are still watching and learning. They will learn how to talk to their own children and their future spouse by watching and listening to you and how you talk to them and your own spouse. How often have you heard your child say something and you smile, because it is a phrase you always use? For example, "I am going to count to three," or maybe your child is playing with dolls and tells one doll, "You must share." These are your words coming through your child.

You certainly don't want the wrong words to be repeated. It isn't always curse words that can make you cringe. It is those phrases and variations that come through. When the kids are playing with their friends, talking to their teachers or fostering relationships, the words you have given them through your own verbal interactions are the words they will use. Teenagers are, of course, going to develop some of their own sayings and phrases that have been picked up from their peers and things like the television and social media, but you can give them a good foundation by teaching them the right way to communicate.

Words Can't Be Taken Back
While you probably never mean the hurtful words or intend to hurt anybody with your words, it is important to always remember that once said, they cannot be taken back. They are out there. They cannot be unheard. No amount of apologizing or positive words can remove those words. It isn't just the person the words were said to that will suffer. You too, will carry around the guilt and regret of having said something that you can never take back. Always think twice before you say anything in the heat of anger or frustration.

Practice some old-fashioned word control by counting to 10 before speaking when you are really frustrated. Say it in your head and hear the words coming out. Do they hurt? Do you instantly regret saying it in your mind? Give yourself some time to think before you speak and avoid that feeling of guilt. Walk away from a situation and give yourself time to cool down and rehearse what you want to say in a way that isn't attacking or hurtful.

Apologize Yes... Take Words Back No!
There once was a man who told a story about another man that he didn't like. He thought the story was true. When the story spread around town, it utterly destroyed the man. His family, his job and his integrity were all devastated by the rumor mill. He finally had to leave town as a ruined and defeated man.

When the man who told the story discovered that the rumor was false, he realized he had helped to destroy an innocent man with his tongue. He went to his pastor and said, *"I have destroyed a man with my words,"* and he told his pastor the whole story. *"Please,"* he said, *"I am sorry. Can I be forgiven this sin?"*

The pastor told the man, *"Take two pillows, go to the public square and cut the pillows open. Wave them in the air. Then come back."* The man thought it was strange, but quickly went home, got two pillows and a knife, ran to the square, cut the pillows open, waved them in the air and ran back to the pastor.

"I have done all that you asked, may I now be forgiven?"

"Not yet," the pastor replied, *"You must first go back to the square and bring every feather back to me."*

"But, I could never do that, the wind has carried the feathers away!"

"Yes," the pastor said, *"And in like manner your careless words have destroyed an innocent man!"*

You can apologize. You can beg forgiveness. You can even be forgiven by the person you have hurt, but relationships are changed and broken down by hurtful words.

CHAPTER FOUR

STICKS & STONES

*"Watch your tongue and keep your mouth shut,
and you will stay out of trouble."*
— Proverbs 21:23 (NLT)

The Tampa Bay Tribune reported about a devastating situation involving two teen girls being charged with stalking for bullying another teen girl who committed suicide. *"Two girls have been arrested in the death of a 12-year-old Lakeland girl who authorities said committed suicide after being bullied by several girls for nearly a year. Polk Sheriff Grady Judd said the girls, ages 14 and 12, faced charges of felony aggravated stalking that resulted in the Sept. 9 suicide of Rebecca Ann Sedwick, who jumped to her death from a tower at an abandoned concrete plant. Most of the harassment came in the form of hateful messages posted and broadcast on social media sites. "We have to stop this," Judd said. "As a child I was told sticks and stones can break your bones but words can never hurt me. ... Today's words stick because they're printed. And words are as hurtful - and sometimes more hurtful - as sticks and stones.""*

Original story is posted here:

http://tbo.com/news/crime/girls-12-and-14-charged-with-stalking-in-polk-teens-suicide-20131015/.

The hateful words of the two charged teens literally plunged young Rebecca to her death, no less than had the offenders climbed that tower and physically pushed her off. Words are weapons. They are no less potent than the power of a sharp sword or speeding bullet. *"Death and life are in the power of the tongue, and those who love it will eat its fruits"* (Proverbs 18:21 ESV). *"The soothing tongue is a tree of life, but a perverse tongue crushes the spirit"* (Proverbs 15:4 NIV). *"With his mouth the godless man would destroy his neighbor, but by knowledge the righteous are delivered"* (Proverbs 11:9 ESV). *"Hide me from the conspiracy of the wicked, from the plots of evildoers. They sharpen their tongues like swords and aim cruel words like deadly arrows"* (Psalm 64:2-3 NIV). *"Do not let any unwholesome talk come out of your mouths, but only what is helpful for building others up according to their needs, that it may benefit those who listen"* (Ephesians 4:29 NIV).

Words are Weapons

Words are weapons. They are no less potent than the power of a sharp sword or speeding bullet.

Your words have more power than you think. Just as the construction worker has the ability to tear down years of work in just a few short days using a bulldozer, your words can bring a life to a point of discouragement in mere seconds. God commands in Ephesians 4:29 (KJV), *"Let no corrupt communication proceed out of your mouth, but that which is good to the use of edifying, that it may minister grace unto the hearers."* God wants your words to minister to those who hear them. He desires for your speech to be uplifting and edifying, rather than derogatory and hurtful. Are you guilty of using hurtful comments, off-handed jokes, and disparaging remarks? Are you a builder or a wrecker? Do your words minister to those who hear them? Or are others often hurt by what you say? Use the tools of compliments, encouragement, edification, and godly speech to build others up.

Contrary to the saying `Sticks and stones may break my bones but words will never hurt me,' words have power and can remain with an individual a long time after they are spoken. This is particularly so for the mind of a young person who is still trying to find their place in society. It is for this reason that parents need to be careful of what they say to their children as they might unknowingly pronounce a curse over their lives. Many lives have been ruined as a result of a careless remark from one who should have known better. Young people are particularly vulnerable to getting hurt through words since they tend to take in most of what is said to them as truth – especially when it comes from their parents.

The Bible is clear on the fact that parents need to be careful in the way they relate with their children. Colossians 3:21 (NIV) says, *"Fathers, do not embitter your children, or they will become discouraged."* As a parent it is important that you know the power of the words that you speak over your children. Since you possess the power to either build or break them, more is the reason why only kind words should be heard from your mouth. It is possible for you to chastise your child in a loving manner without leaving them scarred. Remember that you hold a special influence over the lives of your children and that is why they often take in everything they hear from you. If all you pronounce over them is doom, then you should not be surprised when their lives turn out that way.

Man is created in the image of God thus possessing some of His attributes. The whole creation was through the word and that is how everything came into being. This should tell you how powerful words are as they are capable of achieving much in the life of an individual. When used properly, words have the power to build up an individual. On the other hand, when misused they can cause untold suffering in the life of a person. Even though a child might act like they are not affected by these words, the truth remains that they are damaging.

Knowing then the power they wield over the lives of their children, parents should steer off saying negatives words to them. Speak words of affirmation over your children if you want them to succeed in life. You might assume that the young ones are taking it all very well, but you will be surprised to know how much each mean word you say to them pierces their hearts. Since the Bible warns against being a source of bitterness to your child, you need to be careful about this.

Most people live in self-imposed prison as a result of believing some wrong things their parents have said to them. Children will believe anything you say and even carry it through their entire life. When you make it a habit to speak positively into their lives you are laying a good foundation for them to realize their full potential. We are all wired to believe what we often hear around us and that is why it is good to surround ourselves with positive people. A positive word spoken to a child is like a seed sown into their lives. When it is watered with encouragement it has the potential of growing into something big in their life. The opposite is true about negative words too. These are the ones parents should be concerned about as the future of their children relies on the kind of words that are pronounced over them.

If you ask most successful people about how they made it to where they are now, most will tell you that someone with authority over their life spoke a word into it. Most often, this is a parent who believed in them and did not hide that fact from them. There is something about hearing the same thing said often times that releases the power to achieve anything. If positive words have such a huge affect on the lives of our children how much more the negative ones! These carry the power to injure more than anything else. You might have heard it said that some people would rather suffer physical hurt than emotional hurt. The former is easier to heal than the later, which could require years of persistent effort to heal.

The blood of Jesus Christ is sufficient to break all curses spoken over us, but most people struggle since they do not know that they can use it in their lives. It might be more difficult when one is young and not in the full knowledge of the saving grace of God. To save children the trouble, it is wise for parents to sift the words that they speak to them. Make a commitment to uphold your child at all times and you will be well on track to building him up. Even the most unruly one eventually straightens up by receiving love from his parents since it means a lot to him. It is easy for one to make it in life when they know they have someone behind them who loves them unconditionally. How terrible it must be for the children who grow up with no one to speak well into their lives! These ones lack one of the most vital elements that every young person requires to make something of their lives.

When Jesus was on earth he was able to turn situations around by the power of words. Since we too are called by his name, we should emulate him through the correct use of words to bring positive change to those under our care. It is easier to impact someone with words more than anything else, thus their true value cannot be undermined. By taking your role as a parent seriously you will not only be doing what is right in God's eyes but also paving the way for confident individuals. This is something your children will take long into their lives and will have you to be thankful for. No amount of gifts can take the place of the words that you sow into the lives of your children. Be careful of the things you say to them at all times.

Every child craves the love of their parents. When these two people who brought the child into the world say the wrong things to them it causes more pain than anything else. For it is said that the person whom you love most has the biggest ability to hurt you the most. It is up to parents to take the responsibility of building the inner person of their children so that no part of development is left behind. Children who are aware of their parents' love for them will be confident to share love with those around them. It is those who are unsure that cause so many problems in the lives of people around them.

Contrary to the sticks and stones saying, words that are spoken without consideration do indeed hurt even more than is revealed. Take the instance of a child who grows up being put down by his parents. No matter how much little Jonnie tries to catch the attention of these two people who mean the world to him, he fails miserably each time as they barely notice him at all. He gets used to being ignored with time and reckons there is no use trying anymore. All his dreams and hopes in life are better kept to himself, he realizes, thus he no longer bothers to share with his parents. Yet these are the people who should in effect push him to achieve what he hopes for in life but are far from doing that. Having to grow up without affirmation from one's parents is disastrous to a child as it wears down their will to achieve. The only thing that could be worse is when parents resort to using abusive or negative words on their children.

While positive words offer hope to a child and motivate him to be an achiever, nothing good comes of negative ones. Remember that children view their parents as the most influential people in their lives. The fact that they look up to them means that they believe everything they say to them. When negative words are repeated often to a child by his parents with time they become ingrained in his mind and he starts to believe them. After all, his parents can't go wrong on anything, can they? This particular child then grows up believing the names his parents have placed on him and begins to act that way. *"If mom and dad have labeled me stupid then I must really be stupid."* The parents have curtailed progress of the child since he will not be inspired to try out anything useful. The child, who would have made something out of his life, then becomes stuck on what his parents say about him and, if he does not have a close relationship with God, he loses the will to try anything in life.

Imagine all the potential that is locked up in a child like this one that goes untapped for lack of encouragement from his parents. This is nothing short of wasted talent since, unless in the rare case where such a child gets a mentor elsewhere, much of what he could have achieved in life will go to waste. He went down this path because there was no one to edge him on to realize his place in life. This is why it is important for parents to realize the impact of their words in their child's life. Think about it, your words are the bridge on which your children ride to achieve so much in life. If you use them wisely you will have confident children who are aware of the potential they carry inside and have the courage to tap into it. On the other hand, withholding the much needed encouragement will only spell disaster in the lives of these people that God has entrusted into your hands.

Many people who lead meaningless lives have turned out that way since they had no one to urge them on in life. Never underestimate the power of words, especially when they are used to uplift an individual. You have most probably had an experience whereby you met with someone who spoke into your life and changed the circumstances that you were in before. We tend to believe what others tell us about ourselves and affirmation works to get us on the right footing. There is no way that anyone can claim to be unmoved by what others say about them. In the end it matters to them. More so for a child who is still growing up and depends on the views of others in finding his own identity. When he receives demeaning words then he will most likely soak them in with the result that he will turn out exactly as others have branded him.

The bottom line is that parents need to realize their God-given ability to nurture their children. Raising well-adjusted individuals involves bringing out the children's' potential in the way parents speak to their children. Nothing is more rewarding for a parent than to have their children grow up into individuals who are not shy to pursue their goals in life. This is as a result of the hours that they have sown into offering encouragement to them so as to be able to aspire for more in life. These are parents who seek wisdom from God throughout the journey of walking their children through life's journey with positive affirmation. This is in direct contrast of the ones who view their children in a bad light and do not hide the fact from them. These ones bring up children who are scared to try out anything in life since they already carry with them a negative label from their parents.

Words do hurt and they can badly hurt a child. Only when you as a parent realize this will you do everything to withhold any negative words toward your child and instead seek a better way to air your views. It is possible to tear down a child and leave them bleeding for the rest of their life as a result of careless words spoken to them. Instead, choose to reinforce them with heartening words which act to edge them on to discover the kind of people that God intends them to be. Only then can you stand blameless before God in that you will have done your part in guiding your children into the will of God for their lives.

CHAPTER FIVE

NEVER USE PROFANITY TOWARDS CHILDREN

"Don't use foul or abusive language. Let everything you say be good and helpful, so that your words will be an encouragement to those who hear them." – Ephesians 4:29 (NLT)

Many children the world over have to contend with hearing all sorts of names hurled at them by their parents. It is particularly disturbing when a parent repeatedly uses swear words towards a child. This is demeaning for the child who is left in doubt of his self worth from hearing obscenities hurled his way. Words that have this effect on a child are harmful to them and with time it is likely that the child will also pick them up as well and learn that using these words is acceptable. Nothing is more disturbing than to hear a little one utter a word who barely understands the meaning behind the obscene words they use.

It might seem normal for a parent to curse when, for instance, when they are caught up in traffic. What is said at such a time is quickly absorbed by the child and a parent should not be surprised to hear a repeat of the word from the child later. The parent then has to contend with a taste of his own medicine on hearing the child curse in the same manner. Needless to say, it is nothing to be proud of for a parent as it amounts to a wrong parenting method on their part. Most times younger children have no idea what these words mean, having only heard their parents use them.

Once the word is picked up it becomes difficult to change their vocabulary as they grow older. When a parent notices this trend it is useful that they combat the behavior by admitting a mistake on their part to the child. It is only fair that they admit it is wrong to use curse words and take responsibility since they are responsible for setting a good example for their children. Children take in a lot of what is said to them by their own parents and it is only right for them to model the right behavior to the young ones. Seek for effective ways to communicate with your child so that you do not have to use the four letter words on them at any time. This way you will have saved your child from having to deal with the negative effects of hearing the wrong words hurled at him.

Why Do Parents Use Profanity?

Most parents use profane words towards their children as a way of expressing displeasure. They forget that they are in effect setting pace for their kids to pick up the bad behavior. When you call your child names as a way of letting him know you are not happy with him he takes it to mean that this is the normal way of expressing oneself. It is true that what you say to your child, especially when you are angry, will help him form an opinion about himself. Things that you say to your child out of frustration can leave him feeling unworthy of your love. Be careful not to pass the wrong message to your child, as it will be hard to change the way he sees himself after that. You should explain to a child what they did wrong instead of demeaning them by calling them horrible names. This is the only way for you to avoid causing the child to feel guilty and ashamed.

It hurts them to hear you say something mean to them and – thanks to you – they will likely develop negative feelings about themselves. Demeaning curse words makes a person worthless and they can begin a destructive journey of self-shaming. For a child who is grappling with growing up, this can be an altogether shattering experience to their self-esteem. Most times the use of profanity is meant to show disrespect to the recipient, which is exactly what it does to a child. You can then imagine that this same child will not hesitate to use the same on anyone who crosses them the wrong way. You have started a chain of negative words that will be used either back at you or on others outside your home.

A child who hears his parents use obscene words as a show of disappointment will have a hard time expressing negative emotions. Having learned that cursing is a good way to show how one feels from his parents, he will most likely get in trouble with others outside the family. The child will be forced to deal with the negative impact of swear words at school or elsewhere. Remember that swearing in a child is taken as wrong upbringing by his parents. Do not allow your child to suffer due to your careless and idle words. You will not only have secured his esteem, but also his future relationships with others outside your home.

Relationship Pitfalls from Growing Up with Profanity

When others view your child as having been brought up in the wrong manner, it is most likely that they will hold him in the wrong light too. This does have an impact on him as he could get into trouble through no fault of his. Most people are intolerant of children who curse if they learn it from a parent and it is a destructive path to lead a child down. One of the effects of this is that the child might have trouble forming meaningful relationships with other people. Since swearing might be the only way he knows how to express himself, he could be met with stoic resistance from others who hold a different view. Most of the time a child like this faces alienation at a time when forming relationships is very important to him. Parents need to realize the effect that profanities have on the ability of their children to fit in with others effectively. It is like the use of such is a ticket for your child to be the odd one out in most social settings.

Ephesians 4:29 (NIV) says, *"Do not let any unwholesome talk come out of your mouths, but only what is helpful for building others up according to their needs, that it may benefit those who listen."* The Bible is careful to point out that your words should be used to build up others. It is clear that using abusive words on your child will have the opposite effect on him while adding no value to him. Since you want to bring up a child who is able to add value to the rest of society, it is your role to ensure that only the right words come out of your mouth. Then will not be accountable for setting the wrong example to your child through the use of bad language. Your child will be better able to form close relationships with others around him when only worthy talk proceeds from his mouth, something he can well learn from you.

When a young one has problems with dirty words he is likely to be unsure of the way to put ideas across to people he encounters. This is because what is acceptable to him appears wrong to others. He will grow up devoid of the ability to chart his way concerning important matters of his life, such as a career path since he lacks the knowhow to properly express himself. Yet it is vital that anyone who desires success should be able to articulate his thoughts through the use of the right words.

Be A Good Steward of Your Words

Parents need to be careful not to use words that will interfere with the destiny of their children. Good stewardship means that they should be able to steer clear of anything their children might pick up which is not useful to them. The bottom line is teaching children to be able to express themselves without the need to use abusive words. A child will be able to fit in anywhere as he will be able to aptly express himself to others once this lesson is learned at home. It all boils down to effective communication, something profanity is not able to achieve.

How to Teach Your Children to Express Negative Emotion

Teach your child how to express negative emotion instead of using the wrong words. Parents who abuse their children use the wrong words to show them how they feel. A curse word is an expression of negative emotion that could be put across in a much better manner. Proper expression is what parents should strive to teach their kids and the best way of doing this is by setting a good example. If you are able to deal with negative emotions in a proper manner, then your children will learn from you. You will then be in a better place to correct your child should he pick up swear words from others since you do not use them. It can be difficult for a parent who curses generously in his kids' presence to try to rebuke him when he does the same. Be the kind of person you would like your kids to be as your example is valuable.

Kind Words Build Security

It is a proven fact that parents who use kind words in all situations to their kids bring up secure individuals as opposed to those who use swear words. When a child feels accepted in all situations he will be better able to communicate his feelings. In the event that he picks up such words from other people, it is easy for the parent to correct him when this kind of behavior is alien in their home. On the other hand, it will be hard to correct your child who has learned to use profane utterances from you as a means to get his message across. Since this is something that he has learned from you it becomes even more difficult for him to change when you continue to use them.

Words Can Create a Positive Environment

Parents need to treat their children with dignity, which involves making the right declarations upon their lives. Make the atmosphere within your home one that is conducive for the proper upbringing of confident individuals who will in turn become useful people in the society. Desist from using inflammatory words on your children so that they do not learn the bad habit from you. This way you will be well in the will of God to bring up your children in the right way. They will grow up with fewer problems regarding their self-esteem having had it reinforced in the right manner in your home.

Your kids will have a lot to thank you for when you do everything you can to rear them in a Christian way. The Bible contains all the help that a parent requires in all situations including the proper upbringing of their children. Wise parents read it often to gain useful insights into this very sensitive role.

CHAPTER SIX

WORDS FOR TOUGH TIMES

"Post a guard at my mouth, God, set a watch at the door of my lips." – Psalm 141:3 (MSG)

A group of frogs were hopping contentedly through the woods, going about their froggy business, when two of them fell into a deep pit. All of the other frogs gathered around the pit to see what could be done to help their companions.

When they saw how deep the pit was, the rest of the group, dismayed, agreed that it was hopeless and told the two frogs in the pit that they should prepare themselves for their fate, because they were as good as dead.

Unwilling to accept this terrible fate, the two frogs began to jump with all of their might. Some of the frogs shouted into the pit that it was hopeless and that the two frogs wouldn't have been in that situation if they had been more careful, more obedient to the froggy rules, and more responsible.

The other frogs continued sorrowfully shouting that they should save their energy and give up. The two frogs continued jumping as hard as they could, and after several hours of desperate effort, they were quite weary.

Finally, one of the frogs took heed to the calls of his fellows. Spent and disheartened, he quietly resolved himself to his fate, and laid down at the bottom of the pit, and died as the others looked on in helpless grief.

The other frog continued to jump with every ounce of energy he had, although his body was wracked with pain and he was completely exhausted. His companions began anew, yelling for him to accept his fate, stop the pain and just die. The weary frog jumped harder and harder and – wonder of wonders!

Finally leapt so high that he sprang from the pit.

Amazed, the other frogs celebrated his miraculous freedom and then gathering around him asked, *"Why did you continue jumping when we told you it was impossible?"*

Reading their lips, the astonished frog explained to them that he was deaf, and that when he saw their gestures and shouting, he thought they were cheering him on. What he had perceived as encouragement inspired him to try harder and to succeed against all odds.

This simple story contains a powerful lesson.

"There is life and death in the power of the tongue."

Your Words Matter

Your encouraging words can lift someone up and help them make it through the day. Your destructive words can cause deep wounds; they may be the weapons that destroy someone's desire to continue trying.

Speak life to (and about) those who cross your path. There is enormous power in words. If you have words of kindness, praise or encouragement – speak them now to, and about, others. Listen to your heart and respond openly.

Someone, somewhere, is waiting for your words.

Teenagers Need Your Words of Life

The teen years can be fret with turmoil. Teenagers are uncertain of who they are; they are insecure in a world they don't quite have a handle on. There are bullies and there is peer pressure. Your teens are still learning and growing and don't always have the right words to express how they feel, even when they are feeling the natural stress that accompanies all of our lives. For teens, this stress comes from so much uncertainty. They have to decide what college to go to and/or what to do with their lives. Many of them feel completely vulnerable to the changing winds around them.

It is during these tough times that our teens need us the most. Saying things like, *"I really respect the way you've handled your anger. I know it's not easy"* or *"It really is impressive that you can rise above this situation,"* will affirm to your teens ability to keep striving forward. It says, *"Yes, I know this is a terribly difficult situation,"* and *"Yes, you are handling it in a responsible way."*

Affirming the character of your teens is always important. But affirming their character when the going gets tough is more than just important. It is vital. When your teens are struggling with a situation, when you see them really trying to do what's right in a difficult set of circumstances, you need to affirm that they are, indeed, of strong moral fiber. Whether they would admit it to you or not, they want to be respected for doing the right thing.

As they make the many, many choices find ways to encourage their good choices. You might set aside a regular time to talk about their choices. Call it *Changes and Choices* and promote it as a fun, no-holds-barred time to discuss all the choices they are dealing with. Encouraging them to make the very best decisions and then affirming those choices when they make them can truly change their lives.

And remember not to judge as they discuss the decisions they are facing. Sure, who to go to the prom with may not seem like an earth-shattering choice to you, but it's important to them. And occasionally, especially if you stay with it and allow your teens to discuss what you believe to be trivial, you will stumble across a teen struggling with a choice that will completely define their life path. So listen carefully. When a teen casually mentions that he needs to choose whether to continue to be friends with a group he's not sure he should remain friends with, pay attention. Be there to listen. Be there to encourage a wise choice.

CHAPTER SEVEN

TAMING THE TONGUE

"³ When we put bits into the mouths of horses to make them obey us, we can turn the whole animal. ⁴ Or take ships as an example. Although they are so large and are driven by strong winds, they are steered by a very small rudder wherever the pilot wants to go.⁵ Likewise, the tongue is a small part of the body, but it makes great boasts. Consider what a great forest is set on fire by a small spark. ⁶ The tongue also is a fire, a world of evil among the parts of the body. It corrupts the whole body, sets the whole course of one's life on fire, and is itself set on fire by hell." – James 3:3-6 (NIV)

Do Children Wish they Couldn't Hear?

An elderly man had serious hearing problems for a number of years. His family tired again and again to convince him to get a hearing aid. Finally, he relented. He went to the doctor and was fitted for a set of hearing aids that allowed him to hear 100 percent.

A month later he went back to the doctor. The doctor said with a smile, *"Your hearing is perfect. Your family must be really pleased that you can hear again."*
The old man replied, *"Oh, I haven't told my family yet. I just sit around and listen to their conversations. I've changed my will three times!"*

("Hearing Problems" Crosswalk.com, by Jerry De Luca, Montreal West, Quebec)

How Powerful Are Words?
We know how powerful words are and may keep ourselves in check when we know someone with authority is listening. What about when no one is around to keep you in check? Is it really that bad to lose your temper and say something to blow off steam? Does it really matter if you complain about your spouse to your children? Who cares about what you say to get your kids to move quicker in order to leave the house on time? Children are like the old man before he could hear. They may not truly know what's going on around them or understand the impact, but they will fully understand when they are

older. Just like the old man who could finally hear, children may never let you know how much the words hurt from when they were growing up. Many times parents say things out of habit. They don't really mean what they say, but intentional or not, the words still sting.

How Do You Tame Your Tongue?

What can a parent do about this? The answer is to tame the tongue. James chapter 3 speaks about the power of the tongue. A parent may be copying exactly what their parents said to them, but God can instill the power within you for self-control and guide you to changing.

Here are some practical ways to taming the tongue:

- Do not say anything when you are angry or upset – let the anger cool first.
- Remind yourself that running a few minutes late is momentary, but spewing cutting words is permanent.
- Give yourself at least 10 seconds to think about how you should respond in a situation.

- Ask yourself if what you want to say is coming from a place of love and offering an example of giving grace.
- Ask yourself if what you want to say is actually necessary.
- Think about how you can turn the situation into a learning moment instead of a spewing moment.
- Look at the face of your children and imagine what Jesus would say to them.

Taming the tongue is not easy and it requires tremendous work and patience with your children and yourself. A key to taming the tongue is to fall back on truth. You can point out the truths in a situation and open a conversation to discussion without pointing fingers, blame and casting stones (i.e. spewing death words). In Matthew 5:37 (NASB) Jesus said, *"But let your statement be, 'Yes, yes ' or 'No, no'; anything beyond these is of evil."* In other words, there is no reason to add the filler words that tear a child down. Many parents complain about their children making them late and may yell, *"Why do you always make me late? Can't you just do what I say so we can leave on time?"* Yelling at a child does not motivate them to move faster or teach them how to leave the house prepared and on time, it just instills a fear. A mom could simple say, *"Honey, here are the five things you need to do each morning so you can help us leave on time. Do you remember what those are?"* She could then create a chart for the morning so the child take initiative and she doesn't expend her energy getting frustrated and tearing the child down while neglecting the opportunity to set an important example.

Words of Praise: I Am So Proud of You!

It's great to tell our kids how proud of them you are. But perhaps even more importantly, words of affirmation are about helping kids be proud of themselves. So tell them that. Affirm for them how they should feel about themselves. *"You must be proud!" "You should be proud! How great do you feel about that!"* Saying such things with excitement and cheer will help them understand that they should feel pride within themselves. Being proud isn't something that has to come from others. Helping them find the pride within themselves will help them continue to grow in their self-esteem. It's also a great self-motivator. We like to feel proud of ourselves. It's a feeling that once we've experienced, we want more of.

The more your teens can tap into their own feelings of pride, the less they will worry so much about pleasing others. They'll no longer be quite so apt to succumb to peer pressure, and it will be easier for them to rise above any negative influences in their lives. They will have the self-confidence of knowing they can make the right choices, and they will.

Words of Recognition

Recognition is an essential part of affirming the teens with whom you work. Acknowledging what your teens do goes a long way in showing them that they are appreciated. If they take out the trash or offer to sweep the floor, thank them. Don't let their efforts go unnoticed. Your gratitude/appreciation/affirmation will help them feel that they matter – that they are a significant member of this crazy human race. Let them know what you value, what you respect in terms of behaviors and attitudes. But more than anything, let them know that you appreciate them as people. Provide words of affirmation for exactly who they are.

In our crazy chaotic lives, it's easy to take our teens for granted. They need to know they are valued. Look at each of your teens as a precious jewel that needs attention. Then give each one that attention in your words of affirmation. It is through your words of affirmation that they will begin to see their own self-worth.

Words of Edification and Encouragement

Another principle laid out in the Bible is to use edifying words. Ephesians 4:29 (CSB) states, *"No rotten talk should come from your mouth, but only what is good for the building up of someone in need, in order to give grace to those who hear."* Are your words rotten? If you are not building up, then you are tearing down. It's clear from this verse that as humans, we have many thoughts that enter our minds, but we don't need to share every single thought we have. A maturing Christian thinks through what they are feeling, thinking and then intentionally shares words that are purposeful and meaningful. If you are a parent or someone who works with children, then God chose you for a very important role in His mission. When you start focusing on using words that edify, you also provide a necessary salve from the hurtful words children hear other people use toward them and others.

"May the words of my mouth and the meditation of my heart be pleasing to you, O LORD, my rock and my redeemer." – Psalm 19:14 (NLT)

"Therefore, encourage one another and build each other up – just as you are doing."
– I Thessalonians 5:11 (CJB)

Words not only have the power to hurt they also have the power to help and make us feel good. There's a verse in the Bible that talks about how God wants us to use our words to help others.

I looked up the word "encourage" in the dictionary even though I knew what it meant. Sometimes I'll do that with a word that I already know because it helps me to understand it a little better. The dictionary said that "encourage" means to "give courage, hope or confidence to; to give support to or help."

Words of Kindness

"Kind words are like honey--sweet to the soul and healthy for the body." – Proverbs 16:24 (NLT)

That is the power of encouragement. A kind word, a gracious letter, or an unexpected hug can help someone who is having a difficult time find the courage to continue on. When you want a leader, a child, or someone else to change, then why not encourage them?

"A word fitly spoken is like apples of gold in a setting of silver." – Proverbs 25:11 (ESV)

A word fitly spoken – wow, that must mean that some words are not fitly spoken. All it takes is one word that is genuine and filled with love and grace. Kind words are often short and full of empathy.

Living Out Taming Your Tongue

Here are examples of words of life instead of words of death:

- *"Great job completing all your morning chores on time."*
- *"I knew you could do it!"*
- *"I have confidence that you will do a great job on that test."*
- *"We are running late this morning, so lets work as a team so we aren't late!"*
- *"You are beautiful in whatever you wear."*
- *"Your heart is so tender."*
- *"I love that you took time to say you are sorry."*

Taming the tongue is hard and God knows it can be challenging, which is why He addressed it so many times in the Bible. There are many blessings that come from using a tongue that is tame – it's not just to prevent damaging death words from flying. Here are a few of the many blessings that come from using a tame tongue with children:

- You set an example and expectations of how the children can speak to you and others.
- Children will see that you follow your own rules for speaking kind and building others up.
- You speak truth to the children in your life.
- You teach children to listen out of reverence, not fear.
- Children and teens will be able to see the difference between positive and negative words, which is critical when dating and choosing a future spouse. You can help prevent verbal abuse!
- Kind words open the doors to communication. Prevent the struggle of a teen never opening up to you when they need guidance.
- Children and teens will feel accepted.

CONCLUSION

WORDS CAN INSPIRE GREATNESS

On May 25th, 2011 when the curtain fell on the greatest talk show of all time, Oprah Winfrey, who is the most successful woman in television, singled out one person to thank for making her dream a reality. Out of the 4,561 editions of the *Oprah Winfrey Show* that aired, when it came time to say good-bye she began to reminisce about being a little rural black girl from Mississippi and the specific teacher that she attributed to helping her become what she is. According to Oprah, *"Mrs. Duncan my fourth grade teacher was my first true liberator who made me feel that I mattered."* Oprah goes on to explain that Mrs. Duncan was one of the first people who believed in her. Oprah recalls words of affirmation that she heard from this teacher:

- *"You are just the smartest little black girls I've ever seen!"*
- *"You can take on the world Oprah!"*
- *"You are such a good reader! Your peers love to hear you read!"*

According to Oprah this lady is the reason she had a talk show.

NOTES
THE TONGUES OF CHRISTIAN PARENTS

"Those who consider themselves religious and yet do not keep a tight rein on their tongues deceive themselves, and their religion is worthless."
– James 1:26 (NIV)

Alexander Haig, a U.S. Army general, Secretary of State and White House Chief of Staff, said, *"Practice rather than preach. Make of your life an affirmation, defined by your ideals, not by the negation of others. Dare to the level of your capability then go beyond to a higher level."*

The whole point of using words of affirmation with you young people is to help them overcome whatever internal self-sabotaging, negative feelings they might carry about themselves. Because these young, uncertain years are so tough, kids tend to question nearly everything about who they are and whether or not they are who they're supposed to be. They are filled with doubts. Helping kids to develop their own affirming beliefs is essential.

You will not always be there to provide the encouragement your child needs as a parent. Helping them learn to visualize success and to believe in themselves will leave them with ever-lasting traces of your love and support long after you are gone.

Made in the USA
San Bernardino, CA
04 August 2016